Frank's My Name

Brenda Short

This is a work of fiction. Any reference to people, places or events are creations of the author's imagination and any resemblance to actual events, places or persons living or dead is entirely coincidental.

Library and Archives Canada Cataloguing in Publication

ISBN 978-1-0691530-0-5 (pbk)

Short, Brenda, author

Frank's My Name / Brenda Short

Illustrated by Microsoft AI

Published by Doonhamer Publishing 2024

Dedication

This book is dedicated to my grandchildren

Children's books by this author

1. The Cherry Pie Incident
2. Noel and Sherlock
3. I'll Fix That Cat Later!
4. The Christmas Surprise
5. Frank's My Name
6. The Empty Nest
7. Easter Bunny Has a Fever
8. The Fishing Trip

Preface

Frank is a rabbit with an unusual name. He is bullied constantly by the other rabbits and has no friends because his name is different.

One day, he comes to the aid of the bully who is trapped in a snare.

Frank releases him from the hunter's snare and saves him from the stew pot. They become best friends.

Frank's My Name

All was at peace with the world, and there was excitement in the warren when the mother rabbit gave birth to her latest litter of four kittens, but she was faced with a dilemma. What to name the latest kits.

She soon decided on names for three of them, but that left her little boy kit without a name.

When she asked her mate to help out, he was just as conflicted as she was. What would he name his little son?

All of the cute names were gone. They had used them already for previous litters, Thumper, Cottontail, etc.

Most of the names that they could come up with were too feminine for a boy kit, and he would be teased by the other rabbits.

“This is a difficult thing to decide,” said the father rabbit. “Your name stays with you all your life. We better choose carefully.”

The father rabbit decided that the best thing to do was to ask the rabbit counsel for advice. Surely one of them could come up with an appropriate name.

"Thrasher," said one aggressive male, who practiced Karate.

"Shredder," said his best friend who watched too much Netflix.

"Sailor," said a third, who was involved in amateur dramatics.

"I won't have him going through life with a name like Thrasher or Shredder," said the mother adamantly. "He won't have any friends. Everyone will be scared of him."

“I don’t like the name sailor either,” said the father.

And so they were still no closer to finding a name for their son.

"Why don't you call him Frank?" said one of the elders, causing an explosion of laughter from the rest of the group.

“Frank! What’s a Frank?” asked the mother.

“Frank is not a what. Frank is a who,” said the elder. “I’ve heard that name in the forest. It’s a human name.”

“Well,” said the father, “It’s not tough. It’s not a common name either. Alright, his name is Frank.”

And so, the baby rabbit grew up, the only one amongst all of the other rabbits with a human name.

Anytime Frank did wander out among the group, he was teased and bullied mercilessly, causing his mother to finally admit, “I wish we had called him Shredder. Then they would all leave him alone.”

However, because of this he had no friends and he eventually became a recluse, still living at home when he should have found himself a mate.

But Frank was the one who had to live with it.

He had a name that everyone made fun of, and he hated his name. After all, he hadn't asked to be different from everyone else.

He grew to be one of the biggest rabbits in the warren, and tried to join in with the others in feats of strength, designed to attract a desirable female.

But the others ganged up on him, and drove him away making fun of his name. Would it never end?

Unbeknown to Frank there was one young female, the prettiest and most sought after, that had observed how big and strong he was and she was waiting for him to notice her.

He was so different from the others, shy almost, and his name was magnificent and so unusual.

She didn't mind this. Wasn't he the same as everyone else after all, so why did his name matter so much to everyone.

Snuggles, as she was called, became impatient when it seemed that he wasn't paying attention to her flirts.

She didn't know that he had his eye on her for such a long time, but thought that he would never have a chance with this little beauty. He was resigned to remain a bachelor.

Snuggles gave up on waiting however, and asked him point blank if he was always going to live at home with his parents, or was he looking for a partner to settle down with, making sure he knew that she was looking too.

Frank was overjoyed, but once he had time to think about it, he rejected the idea.

If he were to become her mate she would lose all her friends, and their children would be outcasts all because of his name.

But she wouldn't give up and vowed to meet with him in secret.

However, something happened that afternoon that would change their lives forever.

Sounds of distress were resounding all through the forest. At first it was hard to figure out where they were coming from, and who or what was making those sounds.

Someone was in pain and needed help. But the agonizing cries were coming from outside the long grass at the side of the forest path.

Nobody ever went near the path. That's where the humans lived.

They had guns, and they laid traps to catch unsuspecting rabbits and other forest animals destined for the stew pot.

One of the first things you learned as a kit was not to walk on the path where they could see you.

But Frank thought of himself as immortal in a way. After all, he had a human name and that must give him some kind of immunity.

Humans didn't name their farm animals with human names. So they wouldn't want to eat a Frank, would they?

When Frank reached the edge of the path, the wails were much louder. He soon found the unfortunate creature that had been snared by a paw in a hunter's crude trap.

Lo and behold, this was Thumper, the rabbit that had been his most relentless persecutor all the time Frank was growing up.

Thumper was a reckless individual that took far too many chances to impress the females, and here was a prime example of his carelessness.

He had wandered right into a snare and instead of trying to chew his way out, he just gave in to it and began to cry out.

He wasn't so tough now, it seemed.

"Be quiet, will you?" said Frank, circling the snare. "If you hold still, I'll try and release you."

Obviously, upon closer inspection, the would-be human hunter was inexperienced and the snare wasn't that reliable, but Thumper hadn't taken the time to notice that.

Within moments, Frank had freed him. Thumper would have a bruise on his paw, but nothing was damaged enough to worry about.

“Thank you Frank, but why did you help me? I’ve been the worst bully,” Thumper asked. “I didn’t deserve your help.”

"Why wouldn't I? We're all brothers aren't we?" Frank answered, as Thumper limped into the tall grass and out of danger.

As a result of that day, Thumper and Frank were the best of friends, and the rest of the colony stopped teasing Frank about his name at last.

He was a hero who had saved his worst enemy Thumper from the stew pot.

Snuggles was so proud of Frank, and he finally agreed that they could be seen in public as a couple. Soon they were mated, and soon after that she was expecting her first litter of kits.

One night, when they were huddled together in their burrow, Snuggles asked Frank, “What will we call the babies when they’re born?”

“Anything,” he said, “as long as it’s not Frank!”

www.ingramcontent.com/pod-product-compliance
Lightning Source LLC
LaVergne TN
LVHW021353160826
845679LV00008B/1604

9781069153005